# SEYCHELLES

## TRAVEL GUIDE
## 2024

### DISCOVERING MAHÉ, PRASLIN, LA DIGUE AND ADDITIONAL OUTER ISLANDS

All rights reserved. No part of this publication may be reproduced, distributed, or transmitted in any form or by any means, including photocopying, recording, or other electronic or mechanical methods, without the prior written permission of the publisher, except in the case of brief quotations embodied in critical reviews and certain other noncommercial uses permitted by copyright law.
Copyright ©Alice Lundy,2024.

# TABLE OF CONTENT

Introduction
Chapter 1
    An Overview of Seychelles
    Climate and Geography
Chapter 2
    Making Travel Plans
    Details about Visas and Requirements for Entry
Chapter 3
    Arriving in the Seychelles
    Aircraft and Airports
Chapter 4
    Options for Accommodation
    Exotic Vacation Resorts
Chapter 5
    Island Exploration
    Mahé: The Principal Island
    Praslin: The Peace Island
    La Digue: The Enchanting Island
    Additional Outer Islands
Chapter 6
    Outdoor Excursions
Chapter 7
    Cultural Encounters
    Local Delights and Creole Cuisine
Chapter 8
    Useful Information

Money and Transaction
Chapter 9
　　Sample of Itineraries
Conclusion

# Introduction

The smell of coconut oil and saltwater wafted into the air as I set foot on the white sand beaches of the Seychelles. The sun warmed my skin gently. With every grain of sand beneath my feet, my dream of living in this paradise was realized.

In Mahé, the thriving center of the archipelago, I started my voyage. I was engrossed in the lively Seychelles culture as I meandered through Victoria's winding streets. The vibrant marketplaces were brimming with handcrafted items, spices, and fresh produce, and the pulsating sounds of traditional music filled the air.

Going farther afield, the peaceful embrace of nature provided me with comfort. With its emerald-green peaks and secret waterfalls, Morne Seychellois National Park drew me in and provided a peaceful haven for contemplation and exploration. And I took solace in the gentle sands of Beau Vallon Beach when the sun began to set, losing myself in the captivating dance of the waves.

Yet true enchantment was what I found on the smaller islands. My imagination was captivated by Praslin's luscious forests and immaculate beaches as soon as I arrived. I marveled at the ancient palms and elusive coco de mer nuts that seemed to whisper secrets of a bygone era as I strolled through the ancient Vallée de Mai.

Then there was La Digue, a timeless sanctuary of peace where time passed at a slow pace and bicycles outnumbered cars. I discovered secluded coves and deserted beaches while pedaling along paths shaded by swaying palms, each was more breathtaking than the last. And I knew that this moment would live in my memory forever as I observed the sun set over the famous boulders of Anse Source d'Argent.

I experienced the warmth and hospitality of the Seychellois people all the way on my journey. I experienced a strong bond with this dynamic community through activities like cooking together with local families and learning traditional dances outside under the stars.

Together with memories of the Seychelles' breathtaking scenery and vibrant culture, I reluctantly said goodbye to the island nation, but I also left with a fresh appreciation for the wonders of the natural world. Even though my time in this paradise may have come to an end, I was aware that its spirit would continue to exist inside of me, igniting dreams and new experiences.

# Chapter 1

# An Overview of Seychelles

The 115-island Seychelles archipelago in the Indian Ocean is well-known for its stunning natural beauty, lively culture, and unrivaled peace. Seychelles is a paradise on earth that is northeast of Madagascar on the eastern coast of Africa. It draws tourists from all over the world who are looking for a way to escape to immaculate beaches, verdant jungles, and crystal-clear waters.

The Seychelles' islands are separated into two main groups: the Outer Islands, which are made up of secluded islets and low-lying coral atolls, and the Inner Islands, which are granitic and mostly mountainous. The coral islands offer long beaches and a wealth of marine life, while the granite islands have dramatic landscapes with tall peaks, dense forests, and massive granite boulders.

African, Asian, European, and Creole customs are just a few of the many threads that make up the rich tapestry that is Seychelles culture. Warm and hospitable, the Seychellois take great pride in their multicultural background. The official language of the islands is Creole, which reflects the rich linguistic fusion of African, French, and English elements. However, English and French are also widely spoken.

Tourism, fishing, and offshore financial services are the main drivers of the Seychelles' economy. The islands' immaculate beaches, rich marine life, and opulent resorts attract tourists, who play a crucial role in the economic development of the nation.

The Seychelles is a paradise that provides a special fusion of scenic beauty, cultural diversity, and natural wonders. Indulging in lively Creole culture, exploring verdant jungles, or relaxing on quiet beaches—the Seychelles offers an experience that will make you want to go back time and time again.

# Climate and Geography

Northeast of Madagascar in the Indian Ocean is the archipelago known as Seychelles, which is made up of 115 islands. There are two primary groupings of islands: the Inner Islands and the Outer Islands. With lush greenery, granite peaks, and breathtaking beaches, the Inner Islands are primarily mountainous and granitic. Among the biggest and most popular islands in this group are Mahé, Praslin, and La Digue. However, the Outer Islands are made up of isolated islets and low-lying coral atolls. They have beautiful beaches, an abundance of marine life, and great diving and snorkeling spots.

All year long, the Seychelles experience warm temperatures and high humidity due to its tropical climate. The wet season and the dry season are the two distinct seasons that the archipelago experiences. Most of the islands' yearly rainfall falls on them between November and April, which is known as the wet season. The rich vegetation thrives during this time, and there are frequent but short showers. Cooler temperatures and refreshing southeast trade winds are features of the dry season, which runs from May to October. Because of the generally sunny and dry weather, which is perfect for outdoor activities like hiking, snorkeling, and beachcombing, this is thought to be the best time to visit the Seychelles.

Owing to the islands' varied topography, Seychelles has a variety of microclimates, each with distinctive qualities of its own. Elevations above sea level bring with them cooler temperatures and more precipitation, while coastal regions are typically warmer and more humid. The southeast trade winds act as a natural air conditioner, bringing about a slight drop in temperature and fostering pleasant outdoor exploration circumstances.

Seychelles is susceptible, like many island nations, to the negative consequences of climate change, such as increasing sea levels, acidification of the ocean, and extreme weather. In order to lessen the effects of climate change, the Seychelles government has put in place programs for renewable energy, sustainable development, and coastal protection.

# Chapter 2

# Making Travel Plans

Prepare to realize the dreams you have of the Seychelles! The Seychelles are calling your name with their immaculate beaches and lush jungles. However, let's arrange your ideal retreat before you take off for paradise. Find out when is the best time to go, look for hidden treasures, and prepare your belongings for an amazing trip. The Seychelles offers it all, whether your goals are adventure, relaxation, or cultural immersion. So let's design your ideal schedule and set out on an adventure of a lifetime.

### The Ideal Time to Go

To get the most out of your trip to this tropical paradise, you must pick the ideal time to visit the Seychelles. The archipelago experiences year-round warmth and pleasant weather, but different traveler types benefit from different times of year.

The Arid Period, the best time to visit the Seychelles is generally regarded as the dry season, which runs from May to October. Outdoor activities are more comfortable and pleasurable during this time of year due to the islands' cooler temperatures and revitalizing southeast trade winds. For those who enjoy hiking, beachcombing, and water sports, now is the perfect time to discover the breathtaking scenery and immaculate beaches of the Seychelles without having to worry about torrential downpours.

The wet season, the Seychelles experience higher humidity and warmer temperatures during the wet season, which runs from November to April. This is when it rains more often, but the showers are usually brief and are followed by bright skies. A great time for nature enthusiasts and photographers to capture the Seychelles' breathtaking natural beauty in full bloom is during the wet season, which is marked by lush vegetation and vivid blooms.

The ideal time to travel to the Seychelles ultimately depends on your individual interests and preferences. The Seychelles has something to offer every traveler all year long, whether they are looking for sunny skies and soft breezes or lush landscapes and colorful blooms.

# Details about Visas and Requirements for Entry

It is essential that you familiarize yourself with the entry requirements and visa information prior to traveling to the Seychelles' picturesque islands in order to guarantee a hassle-free and seamless arrival. Comprehending the entry protocols is essential to guaranteeing that you have an unforgettable time in this tropical paradise, be it for an exciting eco-tour, a romantic honeymoon, or a laid-back beach getaway.

The easy visa requirements are among the best things about traveling to the Seychelles. For citizens of many nations, including the US, UK, Canada, and the majority of EU members, the country grants entry without the need for a visa. The Seychelles does not require a visa for visitors from these nations to stay for up to 30 days. For those looking for a hassle-free vacation, this makes the Seychelles an appealing destination.

Convenient visa on arrival is provided by Seychelles for visitors from nations that aren't allowed entry without a visa. In the event that they fulfill specific requirements, this permits travelers to acquire a visa at Seychelles International Airport. These usually include proving you have enough money for the duration of your stay, proving you have onward travel arrangements, and possessing a valid passport that is valid for at least six months after the date of entry. Officials from immigration assist travelers upon arrival, and the visa on arrival procedure is quite simple.

A stress-free and pleasurable trip requires knowing the Seychelles entry requirements and visa information. Having the right paperwork in place will guarantee that you can take advantage of everything the Seychelles has to offer, whether you're planning a quick trip or a longer visit. Seychelles promises to be a unique travel destination for people from all over the world with its breathtaking beaches, lush landscapes, and lively culture.

## Health and Security Advice

Experiencing the splendor of immaculate beaches, verdant jungles, and lively cultures can be had by visiting the Seychelles. A memorable and pleasurable trip, however, depends critically on your health and safety. If you're planning a trip to the Seychelles, take into account the following thorough health and safety advice:

## Ahead of Travel

Medical Examination, it's a good idea to get checked out medically before you travel to make sure you are well enough to go. In order to get any required immunizations or prescriptions, speak with your healthcare provider about any pre-existing medical conditions.

Coverage for Travel, invest in comprehensive travel insurance that will protect you against unanticipated events, medical emergencies, and trip cancellations. As medical evacuation may be required in isolated areas of the Seychelles, make sure your insurance policy covers this kind of evacuation.

Prescription Drugs, in case you need prescription drugs, make sure you have enough for the whole trip. Prescription copies and medication should be packed in their original containers and carried on with your carry-on bags.

## Throughout Your Journey

Remain Hydrated, drink lots of water throughout the day to stay hydrated because the Seychelles' tropical climate can get quite hot and muggy at times. Drinking too much alcohol and coffee can cause dehydration, so limit your intake of these substances.

Sun Protection, wear high-SPF sunscreen, a wide-brimmed hat, and protective clothes to shield yourself from the sun's harmful rays. Try to find shade between 10 a.m. and 4 p.m., when it's the hottest of the day.

Insect Protection, especially in areas where mosquito-borne diseases like dengue fever and chikungunya are common, take preventative measures to avoid mosquito bites by sleeping under mosquito nets, wearing long sleeves and pants, and using insect repellent containing DEET.

Safety in Water, swimmers and those who enjoy water sports should use caution when swimming. Avert rip tides and strong currents by swimming only in approved areas where lifeguards are on duty. Be sure to always follow safety procedures and go with a certified guide if you decide to go diving or snorkeling.

Discovering the natural beauties and cultural treasures of the Seychelles can be an enjoyable and worry-free experience if you heed these health and safety advice. Make your health a top priority, maintain your vigilance, and confidently and calmly enjoy the Seychelles' natural beauty.

# Chapter 3

# Arriving in the Seychelles

Set out for the Seychelles, a paradise waiting for you! The excitement for an incredible journey will begin the moment you step onto a luxury yacht or onto the tarmac of Seychelles International Airport. Whether you're flying through the clouds or sailing across the glistening Indian Ocean, getting to the Seychelles is an adventure in and of itself.

The sight of lush green islands surrounded by turquoise waters will mesmerize you as you approach this tropical oasis. Sail towards your ideal destination and experience the soft sea breeze caressing your hair and the warmth of the sun on your skin.

The Seychelles provide countless chances for adventure and leisure, such as snorkeling with vibrant fish in glistening lagoons, exploring immaculate beaches, and hiking through lush jungles.

# Aircraft and Airports

An archipelago of 115 islands in the Indian Ocean, Seychelles is well known for its breathtaking natural beauty and lively culture. Seychelles' immaculate beaches, verdant rainforests, and abundant marine life attract tourists from all over the world. Seychelles offers a number of airports and airlines with both domestic and international flights, making travel to and from the island nation easier.

**The Seychelles International Airport (SEZ)**, located on the island of Mahé, Seychelles International Airport serves as the main entry point to the archipelago. Seychelles' largest airport, SEZ, acts as a hub for both local and international travel. Modern amenities found at the airport include restaurants, duty-free stores, car rental agencies, and currency exchange desks.

**Flights from Seychelles International Airport**

Air Seychelles, the country's flag carrier, connects Seychelles to locations in Africa, Europe, and the Middle East via both domestic and international flights.

Emirates, with flights to the Seychelles from its hub in Dubai, Emirates offers easy connections for visitors from Asia, Europe, and other regions.

Etihad Airways, with flights to the Seychelles from its Abu Dhabi hub, Etihad Airways allows travelers from Africa, Asia, and Europe to connect easily.

Qatar Airways, with flights to the Seychelles from its hub in Doha, Qatar Airways provides easy connections for visitors from Asia, Europe, and Africa.

**The airport at Praslin (PRI)**, Seychelles' second-biggest airport is Praslin Airport, which is situated on the island of Praslin. Along with chartered flights to other islands in the archipelago, its main functions are serving domestic flights between Mahé and Praslin. The Vallée de Mai Nature Reserve and Anse Lazio Beach, two well-liked tourist destinations, are both conveniently close to the airport.

There are a number of smaller airports and airstrips dispersed throughout the archipelago in addition to Praslin Airport and Seychelles International Airport. Airports on islands like Denis, Bird, and Fregate are among them, along with smaller airstrips that service outlying resorts and private islands. Domestic flights, charter flights, and private aircraft are the main users of these smaller airports.

Seychelles International Airport is the primary entry point for foreign visitors, making air travel the most practical and well-liked method of getting to the islands. Seychelles provides a variety of flight options to meet the needs of every traveler, including both domestic and major international airlines. The airports and airlines of the Seychelles guarantee a smooth and delightful travel experience for tourists from all over the world, whether they are traveling to the main island of Mahé or exploring the immaculate beaches of Praslin.

## Within Seychelles Transportation

With its breathtaking natural scenery and varied attractions dispersed throughout several islands, Seychelles provides a range of transportation choices to enable visitors to fully enjoy its splendor.

**Internal Air Travel**, between the three main islands of Mahé, Praslin, and La Digue, domestic flights are a convenient and well-liked mode of transportation. Regular flights are offered by Air Seychelles to smaller airports and airstrips throughout the archipelago in addition to flights between Praslin Airport on Praslin island and

Seychelles International Airport on Mahé. Travelers can make quick and easy connections on these flights, which also offer breathtaking aerial views of the islands.

Ferreries, the main islands of Mahé, Praslin, and La Digue can be reached by ferry, which provides a reasonably priced and picturesque mode of transportation. Regular ferry services are provided by Inter Island Ferry Seychelles between Mahé and Praslin, with additional connections available to La Digue. Views of the Seychelles' lush landscapes and turquoise waters are breathtaking during the ferry ride.

Car Rentals, travelers who want the independence and flexibility to see the world at their own pace frequently choose to rent a car. The main islands of Mahé and Praslin are home to a number of car rental companies that provide a range of vehicles to accommodate various spending limits and tastes. The roads in the Seychelles are usually in good condition and allow for left-hand driving, which makes getting around the islands fairly simple.

Cabs, the main islands of Mahé and Praslin have an abundance of taxis, making them an easy and comfortable way for visitors to get around. At specific taxi stands, you can hail a cab, or you can make arrangements through hotels and resorts. Taxis are a popular option for tourists touring the islands because they provide door-to-door service and are reasonably priced compared to other modes of transportation.

Public Buses, public buses are a cheap and dependable form of transportation for both locals and tourists on the main island of Mahé. Travelers can experience local life and engage with Seychellois people by taking advantage of the bus network, which links the island's main towns and tourist destinations.

Hire Bicycles, on the main islands of Mahé, Praslin, and La Digue, bicycle rentals are offered to visitors looking for a more environmentally friendly and relaxed way to explore the Seychelles. Travelers who ride bicycles can experience the unspoiled beauty of the islands, find undiscovered gems off the beaten path, and take part in an active and healthy form of sightseeing.

The Seychelles gives visitors the flexibility to easily and conveniently explore its stunning landscapes, immaculate beaches, and lively culture thanks to its variety of transportation options.

# Chapter 4

# Options for Accommodation

Experience the best accommodations available in the Seychelles! With options ranging from luxurious beachfront resorts to quaint guesthouses, eco-friendly lodges, and small boutique hotels, we have something to suit every traveler's tastes and budget. Whether you're looking for a family-friendly getaway, a romantic getaway, or a solo adventure, our lodgings offer convenience, comfort, and life-changing experiences. Experience the tranquil sound of waves lapping against the coast, lose yourself in verdant tropical gardens, and decompress in elegance amidst breath-taking island vistas. With individualized attention, first-rate facilities, and breathtaking scenery, you can easily book your ideal stay in the Seychelles. In this paradise, savor luxury, discover breathtaking natural features, and make lifelong memories.

# Exotic Vacation Resorts

Some of the most opulent resorts in the world can be found in the Seychelles, a country well-known for its immaculate beaches, turquoise waters, and verdant surroundings. Connoisseurs can enjoy unrivaled comfort, flawless service, and breathtaking natural beauty at these exclusive retreats.

North Island, home to uber-exclusive resorts that serve even the most discriminating guests, is a byword for luxury. These resorts provide luxurious villas with private beaches, abundant vegetation, and attentive service. Indulgent spa services, fine dining, and a variety of outdoor and water sports are available to guests.

A private island paradise, Fregate Island Private provides visitors with a unique and personal island experience. Luxurious villas with private infinity pools, breathtaking views of the ocean, and unrivaled seclusion can be found at the resort. Visitors can take advantage of world-class dining and wellness options in addition to exploring the island's immaculate beaches, verdant forests, and variety of wildlife.

Situated atop a hill with a view of Petite Anse Bay's azure waters, the Four Seasons Resort Seychelles provides opulent lodging surrounded by verdant tropical gardens. Visitors can unwind in roomy villas with private infinity pools, eat at fine dining establishments, and revitalize at the spa perched atop a hill with views of the ocean.

Offering visitors an unrivaled sense of privacy and seclusion, Maia Luxury Resort & Spa is a sanctuary of luxury and tranquility. Every villa has a panoramic view of the ocean, a personal infinity pool, and personal butler service. Personalized excursions, fine dining, and holistic spa treatments are available to guests.

Situated amidst unspoiled natural splendor on the exclusive island of Félicité, Six Senses Zil Pasyon provides visitors with an opulent and eco-friendly sanctuary. The resort offers a variety of wellness experiences, such as yoga, meditation, and holistic spa treatments, as well as roomy villas with private pools and fine dining options.

Seychelles' luxury resorts are the pinnacle of extravagance, providing visitors with an unmatched fusion of unspoiled scenery, attentive service, and top-notch facilities. The luxurious resorts in the Seychelles promise an amazing getaway in paradise, whether you're looking for remote seclusion, all-inclusive wellness programs, or immersive nature experiences. At these upscale retreats, indulge in luxury, take in the breathtaking scenery of the Seychelles, and make lifelong memories.

## Boutique Hotels

In addition to its stunning natural beauty and immaculate beaches, the Seychelles is home to a number of quaint boutique hotels that provide guests with a personalized and intimate stay. These boutique hotels provide guests a one-of-a-kind and unforgettable stay by fusing distinctive design elements with opulent amenities.

Le Domaine de l'Orangeraie is a boutique hotel that combines modern and Seychellois architecture, and it's situated on the beautiful island of La Digue. The resort offers guests a tranquil and private haven with roomy villas and suites tucked away amid lush tropical gardens. Le Domaine de l'Orangeraie features a gourmet restaurant serving Creole cuisine, an infinity pool, and a spa, offering the ideal combination of luxury and authenticity.

The H Resort Beau Vallon Beach is a boutique hotel with a touch of tropical elegance, located on the gorgeous Beau Vallon Beach on the island of Mahé. The resort offers a variety of dining options, including a restaurant and bar on the beach, as well as opulent rooms and suites with contemporary amenities. Luxurious spa treatments, water sports, and cultural events are available to visitors, which makes it the perfect option for discriminating vacationers looking for a classy island escape.

Guests can enjoy a boutique hotel with breathtaking ocean views at the Carana Beach Hotel, which is situated atop a charming hillside with a view of Carana Beach's turquoise waters on Mahé. The hotel has a beachfront restaurant serving fresh seafood and regional fare, as well as elegantly furnished rooms and suites with private balconies or terraces. Travelers looking for peace and quiet can find it at the Carana Beach Hotel, which offers a personalized welcome, a laid-back atmosphere, and an emphasis on sustainability.

Constance Ephélia Seychelles is a five-star boutique resort set amid immaculate beaches and lush tropical gardens on Mahé's northwest coast. The resort features a variety of dining options, including fine dining restaurants and beachside bars, as well as spacious suites and villas with modern design elements. It's a great option for singles, families, and couples because it offers a wide range of recreational activities, such as tennis, yoga, and nature walks.

The Seychelles' boutique hotels provide a distinctive fusion of luxury, charm, and individualized care, giving visitors a secluded and genuine island experience. These boutique hotels offer an unforgettable stay amidst the breathtaking natural scenery of the Seychelles, whether you're looking for a romantic retreat, a family-friendly vacation, or a solo adventure. At one of these enchanting retreats, you can indulge in luxury, lose yourself in tranquility, and make lifelong memories.

**Vacation Rentals and Self-Catering Homes**
Guesthouses and self-catering villas provide the ideal balance of comfort, affordability, and flexibility for visitors looking for a more genuine and immersive experience in the Seychelles. These lodgings offer a special chance to experience island life at your own speed, live like a local, and take advantage of home comforts while traveling.

In Seychelles, guesthouses are usually family-run businesses that provide comfortable, reasonably priced lodging in residential areas or picturesque settings. These quaint properties include contemporary guesthouses with cozy amenities as well as classic Creole-style homes. From their hosts, guests can anticipate friendly greetings, attentive service, and insider knowledge of the best places to visit and things to do in the area. Authentic Seychellois cuisine is served in many guesthouses, providing visitors with a taste of the regional specialties and customs.

Villas for Self-Catering, travelers can design their own special Seychelles experience with the freedom and flexibility that self-catering villas offer. These roomy and fully furnished villas are perfect for groups of friends, families, or couples seeking seclusion and freedom while visiting. Self-catering villas provide all the comforts of home, including fully-stocked kitchens, private gardens or terraces, and features like swimming pools and barbecue pits. Visitors can purchase fresh ingredients at neighborhood markets, prepare their favorite dishes, and eat outside while taking in the breathtaking views of the island.

Guesthouses and self-catering villas in the Seychelles provide a distinctive and unforgettable experience. These lodging options offer the ideal starting point for exploring the Seychelles' natural beauty and rich cultural diversity, regardless of your preferences for affordability, authenticity, or flexibility.

**Eco-lodges and Camping**

In the Seychelles, camping and eco-lodges provide visitors with a special chance to fully enjoy the unspoiled natural beauty of the islands while leaving as little of an environmental imprint as possible. Travelers looking for sustainable experiences will find a variety of eco-friendly lodging and camping options in the Seychelles.

In the Seychelles, eco-lodges are often built with environmentally friendly materials and techniques to blend in harmoniously with the natural surroundings. Through programs like waste management systems, solar power, and rainwater collection, these lodges place a high priority on sustainability. In addition to having nice lodging, visitors can lessen their influence on the fragile Seychelles ecosystems.

Intimate connections with nature can be made by campers in the Seychelles. Numerous campgrounds can be found in incredibly beautiful natural settings with breathtaking views of the ocean or dense tropical forests. Campers can enjoy the peace of the Seychelles' natural surroundings while adhering to the Leave No Trace philosophy and showing consideration for the indigenous fauna.

In addition to hiking, snorkeling, and wildlife observation, travelers to the Seychelles can enjoy a variety of outdoor activities while lodging in eco-lodges or camping under the stars. While having an amazing island experience, visitors can support the Seychelles' conservation efforts by selecting eco-friendly lodging and responsible camping.

# Chapter 5

# Island Exploration

Discover the islands of Seychelles' hidden gems! Every island has a different piece of paradise just waiting to be discovered, from the granite wonders of La Digue to the powdery sands of Praslin and the lush jungles of Mahé. Swim in glistening waters rich with colorful marine life, trek through old forests to discover hidden waterfalls, and relax on remote beaches surrounded by towering palms. You will experience stunning scenery, an abundance of wildlife, and friendly Seychellois people at every turn. A memorable getaway is guaranteed on the Seychelles' islands, whether you're looking for adventure, leisure, or romance. So gather your belongings, set out, and take off on a once-in-a-lifetime adventure to this tropical paradise.

# Mahé: The Principal Island

Greetings from Mahé, the bustling capital of the Seychelles! Mahé, the largest island in the archipelago, combines tropical charm, cultural diversity, and breathtaking natural beauty. Discover immaculate beaches bordered by granite boulders, go on hikes through verdant rainforests teeming with rare species, and become fully immersed in the colorful and illustrious culture of the Seychellois people. Indulge in Creole cuisine at hopping markets, find hidden coves where turquoise waters meet sugar-white sands, and go on exhilarating adventures like snorkeling among vibrant coral reefs and climbing to the summit of Morne Seychellois for expansive views of paradise.

Luxurious resorts tucked away along the coast offer world-class amenities and attentive service as you take in the breath-taking views of the ocean. Alternatively, choose for intimate guest houses nestled in quaint villages, providing a genuine Seychellois encounter and gracious hospitality.

Mahé is a world of wonders just waiting to be discovered, not just an island. Mahé offers something for everyone, regardless of whether you're looking for adventure, relaxation, or cultural immersion. So gather your belongings, set your cares aside, and allow Mahé's magic to enchant you.

## Activities and Attractions

The largest island in the Seychelles, Mahé, is a treasure trove of exciting activities, natural wonders, and cultural treasures just waiting to be discovered. Mahé provides a wide variety of attractions and activities to suit every traveler's interests, from vibrant markets and historical landmarks to immaculate beaches and lush rainforests.

Beau Vallon Beach, with its pristine white sands, glistening waters, and lively atmosphere, Beau Vallon is the most well-known beach in the Seychelles. Take part in water sports, swimming, and snorkeling, or just kick back and enjoy the sun while taking in the breathtaking views of the ocean.
National Park of Morne Seychellois, uncover Morne Seychellois National Park, which is home to beautiful hiking trails, uncommon endemic species, and breath-taking panoramic views, as you explore its lush rainforests and misty peaks. For an unforgettable outdoor experience, hike through lush valleys to hidden waterfalls or trek to the summit of Morne Blanc.
Visit the lively Victoria Market, where merchants offer fresh produce, spices, handicrafts, and mementos, to fully immerse yourself in Seychellois

culture. Take in the market's colorful sights, sounds, and scents as you peruse stalls brimming with unique fruits, vegetables, and regional specialties.

Visit the National Botanical Gardens in Mont Fleuri to learn about the unique plants and animals of the Seychelles. Explore verdant tropical gardens, take in the rare palm trees and enormous tortoises, and discover the conservation initiatives underway to preserve the Seychelles' exceptional biodiversity.

Discover the rich history and legacy of Mahé by going to places like Domaine de Val des Près, Mission Lodge, and the Clock Tower. Immerse yourself in the fascinating cultural tapestry of Seychelles by going on cultural tours to learn about the island's customs, architecture, and folklore..

Travelers looking for adventure, relaxation, and cultural immersion will find a multitude of attractions and activities in Mahé. Discovering unspoiled beaches, trekking through rainforests, local markets, and historical sites are just a few of the experiences Mahé offers travelers seeking an incredible journey into the heart of the Seychelles. So gather your belongings, set out on an island journey, and allow Mahé to enchant you with its natural beauty and allure.

## Beaches and Paths for Hiking

The largest island in the Seychelles, Mahé, is endowed with an abundance of breathtaking natural beauty, including gorgeous beaches and verdant hiking trails that entice both adventurers and nature lovers. Whether you're looking for picturesque mountain views or beaches bathed in sunlight, Mahé has a wide range of experiences to offer every kind of traveler.

### Beaches

The most visited beach on Mahé, Beau Vallon Beach is renowned for its immaculate sands, glistening waters, and lively atmosphere. Take part in water sports like jet skiing, scuba diving, and snorkeling, or just kick back and enjoy the sun while sipping cool coconut water from local vendors.

Anse Présentation, a remote haven tucked between dramatic granite cliffs, Anse Intendance provides guests with a spotless beach experience far from the throng. Anse Intendance offers stunning scenery, turquoise waters, and powdery white sands that make it the ideal place for surfing, beachcombing, and tanning.

The lovely beach of Anse Takamaka is encircled by dense vegetation and granite boulders, which give the area a tranquil, isolated feel. With lots of shaded areas beneath the palm trees to rest and unwind, this picturesque location is perfect for swimming, snorkeling, and picnicking.

**Trails for Hiking**
Park National Morne Seychellois, hikers will find paradise in Morne Seychellois National Park, which has a network of beautiful trails that wind through thick rainforests, hazy peaks, and tumbling waterfalls. For sweeping views of Mahé, hike to the top of Morne Blanc. Alternatively, take a tour of the Tea Plantation Trail to discover more about the history of tea production and colonial Seychelles.

The Copolia Trail is a moderate hiking path that ascends Copolia Mountain and provides stunning vistas of Mahé's interior and coastline. Hikers can see endemic plants and animals along the route, such as the uncommon Seychelles pitcher plant and a variety of vibrant bird species.

Trois Frères Trail, hikers who are up for a challenge can venture deep into Morne Seychellois National Park along the Trois Frères Trail, which winds through rocky outcrops, dense forests, and breathtaking vistas. Hikers can take in expansive views of Mahé's coastline as well as the majestic granite peaks known as the Three Brothers.

Mahé's hiking trails and beaches provide a multitude of chances for outdoor adventure and discovery. Mahé promises incredible experiences amidst its natural beauty, whether you're trekking through lush rainforests to panoramic viewpoints or basking in the sun on a secluded beach. So fasten your hiking boots, get your bathers, and set out on an exploration of this tropical haven.

### Historical Monuments and Museums

The largest island in the Seychelles, Mahé, is endowed with a rich cultural heritage that reflects the diverse influences of its people and history in addition to its stunning natural surroundings. Mahé offers an abundance of cultural sites that are just waiting to be discovered, from fascinating museums to lively markets and historic landmarks.

The famous Victoria Clock Tower, a landmark in Victoria, the capital city of Seychelles, is a reminder of the island nation's colonial past. Constructed in 1903, the clock tower bears resemblance to London's renowned Big Ben and is a well-liked location for tourists to capture photographs and appreciate its stunning architectural design.

Located in Victoria, the Seychelles National Museum offers insights into the archipelago's history, culture, and natural heritage. Exhibits highlight the rich biodiversity of the Seychelles, traditional crafts, and people's history through artifacts, photos, and interactive displays.

A restored plantation home from the colonial era, Domaine de Val des Près gives guests a look into the history of plantations in the Seychelles. Discover the lush gardens, exquisitely preserved Creole architecture, and the island's production of spices and vanilla.

With panoramic views and rich cultural significance, Mission Lodge is a historic site perched on a hill overlooking Mahé's west coast. Originally a school for freed slaves, the location now honors the missionaries' contributions and the Seychelles' abolition of slavery.

Take in the lively ambiance of the Sir Selwyn Selwyn-Clarke Market in Victoria, where merchants offer handicrafts, fresh produce, spices, and mementos. Take in the market's commotion as you peruse booths brimming with unusual fruits, vegetables, and regional specialties.

The goal of the Kreol Institute in Victoria is to conserve and advance the distinctive Creole language and culture of the Seychelles. Through exhibits, workshops, and cultural events held at the institute, visitors can learn about Seychellois customs, folklore, music, and cuisine.

A fascinating journey through the rich heritage of the Seychelles, from its colonial past to its vibrant Creole culture, can be had at Mahé's museums and cultural sites. Mahé offers travelers extraordinary cultural experiences, whether they are discovering the island's history and customs, perusing vibrant markets, or touring famous sites.

# Praslin: The Peace Island

Praslin is a fascinating island known for its immaculate beaches, dense forests, and peaceful atmosphere. It is located in the center of the Seychelles archipelago. Travelers from all over the world are captivated by Praslin's natural beauty and serene aura, which makes it the second largest island in the Seychelles. Praslin is the ideal location for rest and renewal for the following reasons, which are summarized in this detailed overview:

The renowned Anse Lazio and Anse Georgette are just two of the stunning beaches in Praslin, Seychelles. These beaches provide the ideal environment for swimming, snorkeling, and sunbathing thanks to their powder-white sands, glistening clear waters, and tall palm trees swinging in the light wind.

Discover Curieuse Island's immaculate beaches, mangrove forests, and enormous tortoise sanctuary by taking a day trip there, which is situated just off the coast of Praslines. Explore the island's rich history and conservation initiatives while hiking beautiful trails and snorkeling in pristine waters.

Nicknamed Côte d'Or Beach, Anse Volbert is a serene beach with turquoise waters and swaying palms. Anse Volbert provides a tranquil getaway from the daily grind and is ideal for swimming, kayaking, and beachcombing.

Visit the towns, markets, and cultural institutions in the area to fully immerse yourself in Praslin's rich history and culture. Get a glimpse of the way of life of the Seychellois by engaging with them, sampling real Creole food, and learning traditional dances and music.

A haven of peace and breathtaking scenery, Praslin enchants the senses and revitalizes the spirit. It is more than simply an island. For tourists looking for a true tropical paradise, Praslin offers a unique combination of adventure, relaxation, and cultural immersion with its immaculate beaches, lush forests, and vibrant culture. Come, then, and let yourself be drawn away to Praslin, where countless wonders await exploration.

## Natural Reserve of Vallée de Mai

Situated in the center of Praslin, Seychelles, is the captivating Vallée de Mai Nature Reserve, which is recognized as a UNESCO World Heritage Site and a vibrant example of the archipelago's natural marvels. This ethereal forest, sometimes called the "Garden of Eden," is home to the famous coco de mer palm tree, a representation of the Seychelles' exceptional biodiversity and the producer of the world's largest seed.

Exploring the historic forests of Vallée de Mai will transport you to a world unspoiled by time. The Seychelles islands' primordial past is brought to life for visitors through towering palm trees, luxuriant undergrowth, and thick foliage, which all combine to create an ethereal and tranquil atmosphere.

Admire the enormous coco de mer palm trees, which are unique to the Seychelles and cannot be found anywhere else on the planet. With their large, double-lobed nuts that resemble a female pelvis, these iconic trees—which can grow as high as 30 meters—have earned the nickname "love nut."

Explore the Seychelles black parrot, vanilla orchids, and pitcher plants, among other uncommon and indigenous plant species, in Vallée de Mai.

Explore beautiful hiking paths that meander through the forest, providing stunning vistas of granite outcrops, towering palm trees, and hidden waterfalls. All ages and fitness levels can enjoy the trails at Vallée de Mai, which let visitors take in the beauty of nature whether they're just taking a leisurely stroll or an intense hike.

The Vallée de Mai visitor center offers interactive exhibits and interpretive displays that shed light on the reserve's significance as a biodiversity hotspot and UNESCO World Heritage Site.

An exceptional chance to witness the wild beauty and age-old charm of the Seychelles' natural heritage is provided by the Vallée de Mai Nature Reserve, a true gem of Praslin. In the center of paradise, Vallée de Mai offers an amazing experience, whether you're admiring the enormous coco de mer palm trees, seeing uncommon wildlife, or just taking in the peace and quiet of the forest.

### Anse Georgette and Anse Lazio Beaches

A blend of natural beauty, tranquility, and serenity, Anse Georgette and Lazio are two of the world's most beautiful beaches, nestled on the northern coast of Praslin Island in the Seychelles. These beaches are a must-visit for tourists looking for a pristine paradise.

**Anse Lazio**

Sapphire Seas and Pristine Sands, a picture-perfect location for swimming, snorkeling, and sunbathing,

Anse Lazio is well-known for its pristine turquoise waters and powder-white sands. Tall granite boulders and luxuriant vegetation envelop the beach, contributing to its picturesque charm.

Diverse and Colorful Marine Life, the rich underwater biodiversity that exists in the waters around Anse Lazio will excite snorkelers and divers alike. Underwater enthusiasts will find themselves in paradise as they explore vibrant coral reefs teeming with exotic fish, sea turtles, and other fascinating creatures.

Magnificent Dusks, Anse Lazio becomes a mystical haven drenched in golden light when the sun sets. Watch as the sun sets to create a romantic ambiance that is ideal for couples and photographers alike. The sky is painted in hues of orange, pink, and purple.

**Anse Georgette**

A Remote Peace of Mind, located on Praslin's northwest coast, Anse Georgette is a hidden gem that can only be reached by foot or boat. It is the perfect place for honeymooners, couples, and anyone else looking for a quiet getaway from the bustle of daily life because this immaculate beach offers seclusion and tranquility.

With its soft white sands, turquoise waters, and lush greenery bordering the shoreline, Anse

Georgette boasts unspoiled natural beauty. Beautiful granite cliffs and lush hills surround the beach, making it a perfect location for picnics and leisurely walks.

Limited Access, only Constance Lémuria Resort guests are permitted access to Anse Georgette, guaranteeing a secluded and unique experience for those who are fortunate enough to go. In addition to water sports and nature walks with guides, guests can take advantage of free amenities like beach loungers, umbrellas, and refreshments.

The beaches of Anse Lazio and Anse Georgette perfectly capture the peace and natural beauty of the Seychelles, providing visitors with a piece of paradise they will never forget. A memorable getaway in the middle of the Indian Ocean is guaranteed by these immaculate beaches, regardless of your preferences for adventure, leisure, or romance. On Praslin Island, Anse Lazio and Anse Georgette offer breathtaking beauty.

## National Park of Praslin

Concealed on the alluring Praslin island in the Seychelles, Praslin National Park is a symbol of the archipelago's dedication to conserving its exceptional natural legacy. This protected area allows visitors to fully experience the unmatched biodiversity and natural beauty of the Seychelles, with its lush forests, immaculate beaches, and diverse ecosystems.

The Vallée de Mai Nature Reserve, a UNESCO World Heritage Site and one of the most recognizable landmarks in the Seychelles, the Vallée de Mai Nature Reserve is located in the center of Praslin National Park. In addition to a wide variety of unique plant and animal species that are unique to this ancient forest, it is home to the fabled coco de mer palm tree. Hiking paths are beautiful, towering palm trees are breathtaking, and uncommon creatures like the Seychelles black parrot and enormous millipedes can be seen by interested parties.

Immaculate Shorelines, Seychelles' most beautiful beaches, Anse Lazio and Anse Georgette, are located in Praslin National Park. Surrounded by stunning natural scenery, these beaches feature powdery white sands, crystal-clear waters, and lush vegetation, providing a tranquil environment for swimming, snorkeling, and sunbathing.

To preserve the distinctive plants and animals of the Seychelles, conservation activities are greatly aided by the presence of Praslin National Park. Invasive species control, habitat restoration, and environmental education initiatives are some of the ways the park works to protect the island's natural heritage for future generations.

Tours for birdwatching, cultural encounters, and guided nature walks are just a few of the ecotourism activities available to visitors to Praslin National Park. These programs encourage environmentally friendly travel habits while offering insights into the Seychelles' rich biodiversity, cultural legacy, and conservation efforts.

A variety of visitor amenities are available at the park to suit the interests and accessibility of visitors of all ages, including picnic areas, hiking trails, interpretive centers, and guided tours. Praslin National Park offers something for everyone, regardless of your interests—nature lovers, thrill seekers, or just someone looking to relax amid the natural beauty of the Seychelles.

Offering guests the opportunity to reacquaint themselves with nature and discover the wonders of the Seychelles' distinct ecosystems, Praslin National Park is a sanctuary of pristine nature and biodiversity. A visit to Praslin National Park guarantees an amazing experience in one of the most stunning locations on earth, whether you're exploring ancient forests, relaxing on quiet beaches, or learning about conservation efforts. So, prepare for a voyage of discovery in Praslin National Park by putting on your hiking boots, packing your swimsuit.

# La Digue: The Enchanting Island

La Digue is a timeless gem that enchants visitors with its rustic charm, immaculate beaches, and laid-back atmosphere. It is nestled within the Seychelles archipelago. La Digue, well-known for its unspoiled beauty and bucolic surroundings, provides a singular fusion of natural marvels and genuine Seychellois culture.

Anse Source d'Argent, Grand Anse, and Anse Cocos are a few of the Seychelles' most picturesque beaches that can be found in La Digue. These beaches provide an idyllic environment for swimming, snorkeling, and sunbathing with their powder-white sands, glistening clear waters, and striking granite boulders.

Discover well-known locations like Anse Source d'Argent, renowned for its unusual rock formations and breathtaking sunsets. Explore the emerald lagoons, secret coves, and verdant coconut groves of La Digue and uncover the natural splendor that has attracted photographers and artists.

Discover the friendliness and warmth of Seychellois culture through engaging with the community, sampling regional cuisine, and becoming fully immersed in the lively way of life on the island.

Discover the rich history and heritage of the island by going to local markets, participating in cultural festivals, and taking guided tours and cultural events.

Explore the coral reefs beneath La Digue, which are brimming with vibrant fish, sea turtles, and other aquatic life. Explore secret coves and underwater caverns, go diving or snorkeling in pristine waters, and get up close and personal with the stunning marine biodiversity of the Seychelles.

La Digue is dedicated to protecting its cultural legacy and scenic surroundings via eco-friendly tourism and conservation initiatives. It is recommended that visitors honor the environment, patronize neighborhood establishments, and engage in eco-friendly pursuits that lessen their influence on the island's fragile ecosystems.

More than just an island, La Digue is a haven of charm, peace, and scenic splendor that invites visitors to relax, explore, and experience the true spirit of the Seychelles. Amid its timeless landscapes and warm Seychellois hospitality, La Digue promises an unforgettable experience whether you're looking for adventure, relaxation, or cultural immersion.

## L'Union Estate

L'Union Estate, a historic plantation offering visitors a unique blend of natural beauty, cultural heritage, and authentic Seychellois experiences, is situated on the enchanted island of La Digue in the Seychelles. Encircled by verdant vistas and steeped in history, L'Union Estate offers an intriguing window into the colonial history and customs of the Seychelles.

French settlers founded the prosperous coconut and vanilla plantation known as L'Union Estate in the 1800s. The estate's well-preserved structures, such as the ox-driven coconut mill, copra kiln, and traditional Creole house, provide visitors with insights into the rich cultural legacy of the island and the plantation era of the Seychelles.

The giant tortoise sanctuary at L'Union Estate, which is home to the Seychelles-native Aldabra giant tortoises, is one of the estate's main attractions. Observing these gentle giants roaming freely in their natural habitat, getting up close and personal with them, and learning about conservation efforts aimed at saving these iconic creatures from extinction are all available to visitors.

Anse Source d'Argent, one of the most photogenic beaches in the world, is also located in L'Union Estate. This gorgeous beach provides an ideal setting for swimming, snorkeling, and sunbathing thanks to its powder-white sands, glistening waters, and striking granite boulders.

Discover the vanilla plantation at L'Union Estate, where traditional methods are used to cultivate and harvest fragrant vanilla orchids. At the on-site craft village, guests can buy locally produced vanilla goods and souvenirs and discover the entire vanilla production process, from pollination to curing.

Take advantage of L'Union Estate's guided tours, cultural shows, and interactive experiences to fully immerse yourself in Seychellois customs and culture. Discover the lively way of life on the island by partaking in activities like palm weaving and coconut husking, as well as by sampling authentic Creole cuisine and attending traditional dance performances.

L'Union Estate offers guests a diverse experience that honors the Seychelles' rich heritage and breathtaking landscapes. It is a treasure trove of history, culture, and natural beauty. Discovering ancient plantations, engaging with enormous tortoises, or simply relaxing on immaculate beaches are just a few of the experiences that L'Union Estate offers when visiting the center of La Digue.

## Anse Source d'Argent

Nestled on the alluring island of La Digue in the Seychelles, Anse Source d'Argent is a timeless marvel of the natural world, enthralling tourists with its immaculate beaches, glistening waters, and imposing granite boulders. Anse Source d'Argent, one of the most widely photographed beaches in the world, provides a paradisiacal scene that perfectly captures the allure of the Seychelles' tropical paradise.

Stunning Scenery, Anse Source d'Argent is home to an incredible landscape with towering granite boulders sculpted by nature, translucent turquoise waters, and powdery white sands. These recognizable boulders form quaint coves, alcoves, and tidal pools that provide an enthralling setting for swimming, tanning, and taking pictures.

Luxurious Beach Feelings, feel the warm sun caressing your skin, feel the soft sands of Anse Source d'Argent beneath your toes, and listen to the tranquil sound of waves gently lapping against the shore to experience the pinnacle of beach bliss. This picturesque beach promises a peaceful getaway from the daily grind, whether you're looking for romance or solitude.

Paradise for Snorkeling and Diving, discover the colorful underwater ecosystem of Anse Source d'Argent, which is brimming with unique fish, coral reefs, and other marine life. Divers and snorkelers can marvel at the kaleidoscope displays of marine life, seeing creatures like moray eels, parrotfish, and butterflyfish in their native environments.

Photography Haven, due to its ethereal beauty, Anse Source d'Argent is a popular destination for artists and photographers who want to capture the essence of the natural landscapes of the Seychelles. The interplay of light, shadow, and texture at this famous beach presents countless opportunities for striking compositions and breath-taking shots, regardless of your level of experience with photography.

Facilities and Accessibility, Anse Source d'Argent is a convenient location for beachgoers and day trippers because it is easily accessible by foot or bicycle from La Digue's main village. The beach has all the necessities, including parking, restrooms, and refreshment stands, to make sure guests have a nice and relaxing time.

Anse Source d'Argent is a sanctuary of natural beauty, peace, and wonder that satisfies the senses and uplifts the spirit. It is more than just a beach. This famous beach offers an amazing journey into the center of the Seychelles' tropical paradise, whether you're relaxing on its immaculate sands, discovering its underwater treasures, or just taking in the breath-taking scenery.

## Veuve Natural Area

Situated on the charming island of La Digue in the Seychelles, the Veuve Nature Reserve is a symbol of the archipelago's dedication to protecting and maintaining its distinct biodiversity. This protected area is named for the paradise flycatcher, or "Veuve," that is native to the Seychelles. It provides visitors with a unique chance to see uncommon bird species, luxuriant vegetation, and unspoiled ecosystems in their natural habitat.

Paradise Flycatcher's habitat in the Seychelles, the primary goal of the Veuve Nature Reserve is to protect the Seychelles paradise flycatcher, an endemic bird species that can only be found on La Digue. The reserve's flagship species, the Veuve, is a representation of the Seychelles' rich natural heritage with its striking black plumage and long tail feathers.

Opportunities for Birdwatching, the wide variety of bird species that live in the Veuve Nature Reserve will delight birdwatchers and nature enthusiasts. It's a birdwatcher's paradise because, in addition to the Seychelles paradise flycatcher, visitors may also see other uncommon and endemic birds like the Seychelles bulbul, Seychelles blue pigeon, and Seychelles sunbird.

Scenic Trails and Lush Vegetation, discover the rich vegetation and beautiful trails that meander through mangrove swamps, dense forests, and coastal landscapes within the reserve. Along the way, guests can take in expansive views of La Digue's breathtaking natural beauty and admire a variety of endemic plant species, such as ferns, orchids, and palm trees.

The Veuve Nature Reserve is essential to conservation efforts aimed at preventing invasive species, habitat loss, and other threats to the distinctive flora and fauna of the Seychelles. The Seychelles paradise flycatcher and other endangered species are the focus of research, habitat restoration, and community outreach initiatives at the reserve.

Visit the reserve's interpretive center to learn about the value of protecting biodiversity and the distinctive ecosystems of the Seychelles. Guided tours, educational programs, and interactive exhibits offer insights into the ecological significance of the reserve and the difficulties faced by the Seychelles' indigenous wildlife.

A haven of biodiversity and breathtaking scenery, the Veuve Nature Reserve gives visitors a unique look at the distinctive ecosystems of the Seychelles and the amazing animals that call them home. The Veuve Nature Reserve in La Digue offers a unique experience whether you choose to hike, go birdwatching, or just spend time in nature. So grab your hiking boots and binoculars, and head to this pristine wilderness sanctuary in the Seychelles for a voyage of discovery.

# Additional Outer Islands

## Silhouette Island: The Unspoiled Paradise of the Seychelles

One of the Outer Islands of the Seychelles, Silhouette Island is well-known for its gorgeous beaches, verdant jungles, and abundant wildlife. It is a pure sanctuary of peace and beauty. Secluded and a peaceful haven from the daily grind, Silhouette Island lies northwest of Mahé and beckons exploration of its pristine scenery and unspoiled wilderness.

Anse La Passe and Anse Lascars, two of the most gorgeous beaches in the Seychelles, are located on Silhouette Island. These uncrowded beaches provide a tranquil environment for swimming, snorkeling, and sunbathing thanks to their powder-white sands, turquoise waters, and swaying palm trees.

Discover the verdant landscapes and lush rainforests of Silhouette Island by hiking along the island's network of trails. Hike through thick vegetation, scale granite peaks, find hidden waterfalls, and reach sweeping viewpoints with views of the surrounding islands and ocean.

Divers and snorkelers frequently visit Silhouette Island because of its diverse array of marine life and coral reefs. In order to preserve the island's delicate ecosystems and encourage environmentally friendly travel, the island's marine conservation initiatives work to safeguard the island's natural beauty for coming generations.

As a recognized wildlife sanctuary, Silhouette Island offers safety to threatened species like the Seychelles giant tortoise and sheath-tailed bat. To see these unusual animals in their native habitat, visitors can go on guided nature walks, birdwatching tours, and wildlife spotting excursions.

Discover the pinnacle of luxury and sustainability at the boutique hotels and eco-friendly resorts on Silhouette Island. Accommodations range from hillside hideaways to beachfront villas, all of which offer visitors a private and ecologically conscious getaway while blending in with the island's natural surroundings.

Silhouette Island is dedicated to sustainability and conservation, working hard to protect endangered species, maintain its natural habitats, and cut down on carbon emissions. In addition to supporting regional conservation initiatives and learning about the distinctive ecosystems and biodiversity of the Seychelles, visitors can engage in eco-friendly activities.

A hidden gem just waiting to be found, Silhouette Island provides visitors with a genuine Seychellois experience amidst pristine beaches and unspoiled wilderness. An amazing journey into the heart of the Seychelles' outer islands is what Silhouette Island promises, whether you're looking for adventure, relaxation, or a closer relationship with nature. So gather your courage and set out on a journey of exploration to Silhouette Island, where paradise is waiting for you around every bend.

## Denis Island: A Calm Sanctuary in the Outer Islands of the Seychelles

Travelers seeking seclusion, unspoiled beauty, and genuine Seychelles experiences are drawn to Denis Island, which is tucked away in the farthest reaches of the Outer Islands of the Seychelles. Denis Island provides a peaceful haven from the stresses of contemporary life, enabling visitors to rediscover themselves and the natural world with its quiet beaches, verdant surroundings, and colorful marine life.

Miles of immaculate beaches line Denis Island's coastline, providing guests with the opportunity to relax on fine white sands and go swimming in glistening waters. The island's quiet beaches offer the ideal setting for rest and renewal, whether you're taking a leisurely stroll along the shore, sunbathing, or having a romantic picnic.

Denis Island, surrounded by colorful coral reefs and brimming with marine life, is a snorkeler's and diver's dream come true. Discover vibrant underwater gardens, come across tropical fish, rays, and sea turtles, and be in awe of the marine biodiversity of the Seychelles in its natural setting.

Denis Island is dedicated to using sustainable conservation techniques to preserve its pristine ecosystems and biodiversity. In addition to participating in eco-friendly activities and supporting local initiatives aimed at safeguarding the Seychelles' natural heritage for future generations, visitors can also learn about the island's conservation efforts.

Situated amidst lush tropical gardens, Denis Island's eco-friendly resort offers guests spacious cottages that offer the ultimate in barefoot luxury. Travelers can expect a tranquil and sustainable getaway from lodgings that blend in perfectly with the island's natural surroundings, from rustic chic interiors to expansive views of the ocean.

Denis Island provides a variety of outdoor activities, such as fishing, kayaking, and paddleboarding, for those looking for adventure. Discover the beauty of the Seychelles' outer islands from a different angle by going on a sunset cruise, cycling along picturesque trails, or exploring the island's mangrove forests.

A haven of unspoiled beauty, peace, and genuineness, Denis Island provides guests with a once-in-a-lifetime chance to get away from the masses and rediscover the spirit of the Seychelles' outer islands. Amid its immaculate landscapes and friendly Seychellois hospitality, Denis Island promises an unforgettable experience whether you're looking for adventure, relaxation, or cultural immersion. Thus, gather your belongings, bid your concerns farewell, and set out on an exploration voyage to Denis Island, where a utopia is waiting around every bend.

## Bird Island: An Outer Island Natural Sanctuary in the Seychelles

Bird Island, a serene retreat from the bustle of modern life, is tucked away in the northernmost part of the Seychelles archipelago. It is a haven of unspoiled beauty and biodiversity. Travelers looking for adventure, relaxation, and a closer connection with nature are drawn to Bird Island, which is well-known for its plethora of birdlife, gorgeous beaches, and vibrant marine ecosystems.

As its name suggests, Bird Island is home to an incredible variety of bird species, making it a haven for ornithologists and birdwatchers. There are countless opportunities for birdwatching and wildlife photography on the island thanks to its diverse avifauna, which includes magnificent frigatebirds, graceful terns, colorful tropicbirds, and uncommon shearwaters.

Apart from its avian residents, Bird Island is also the home of a herd of enormous Aldabra tortoises, a species unique to the Seychelles. Throughout the island, visitors can witness these gentle giants moving freely, marveling at their ancient presence and helping to preserve their natural habitat through conservation efforts.

Some of the most beautiful beaches in the Seychelles can be found on Bird Island, which has private coves, white sand beaches, and turquoise waters. The island's immaculate beaches offer the ideal setting for leisure, whether you're swimming, snorkeling, or sunbathing.

Rich marine ecosystems brimming with life, such as vibrant coral reefs, tropical fish, and sea turtles, encircle Bird Island. Travelers can explore underwater gardens, snorkel or dive in pristine waters, and get up close and personal with the stunning marine biodiversity of the Seychelles.

Bird Island is dedicated to environmentally friendly tourism and sustainable tourism practices as a recognized nature reserve. The island's conservation efforts, renewable energy projects, and eco-friendly lodging all work to reduce its environmental impact and safeguard its scenic beauty for future generations.

Experience the fascinating ecosystems, conservation initiatives, and native fauna of the Seychelles through informative lectures, interactive activities, and escorted nature walks on Bird Island. Gaining knowledge about the island's ecology, natural history, and cultural legacy helps visitors appreciate the Seychelles' abundant biodiversity on a deeper level.

Visitors have a unique chance to experience the pristine landscapes and abundant wildlife of the Seychelles at Bird Island, a sanctuary of natural wonder. Bird Island offers an amazing journey into the heart of the Seychelles' outer islands, perfect for beachcombing, birdwatching, or just relaxing and taking in the island life.

# Chapter 6

# Outdoor Excursions

Take a breath-taking voyage through the outdoor playground of the Seychelles! There is adventure around every corner, from hiking trails through lush rainforests to diving into turquoise waters teeming with vibrant marine life. Experience the exhilaration of ziplining through the treetops, kayaking along immaculate coastlines, and cycling through breathtaking scenery. Climb granite peaks, find remote beaches where time stands still, and explore hidden coves. The Seychelles provides countless chances for outdoor excitement and life-changing experiences, regardless of your preference for extreme sports or peaceful, natural settings.

### Diving and Snorkeling

Seychelles is a top destination for snorkelers and divers because of its breathtaking coral reefs, pristine waters, and variety of marine life. These features have earned Seychelles international recognition. Discover the many underwater treasures that the archipelago has to offer, regardless of your level of diving expertise.

The coral reefs in the Seychelles are among the healthiest in the world, brimming with a rainbow of colors and life. Explore underwater gardens, swim-throughs, and intricate coral formations that are home to a dizzying variety of marine life by diving beneath the surface.

Plentiful Marine Biodiversity, discover the underwater ecosystems of the Seychelles, home to a staggering array of marine species such as vibrant reef fish, sea turtles, rays, and sharks. Dive with schools of tropical fish, see magnificent manta rays, and watch sea turtles glide through the water with such grace.

Sites to Dive at Every Level, divers of all skill levels can find dive sites in the Seychelles, from dramatic drop-offs and underwater seamounts for experienced divers to shallow reefs perfect for novices. There is something for everyone beneath the waves, whether you're looking for shipwrecks in the Indian Ocean or exploring granite formations off the coast of La Digue.

Exclusive Marine Zones, explore the protected marine reserves of the Seychelles, like Sainte Anne Marine National Park and Curieuse Marine National Park, where the preservation of fragile ecosystems is guaranteed by stringent conservation measures.

Excellent snorkeling is available off the coast of Seychelles for those who would rather stay closer to the surface. Discover hidden coves, protected bays, and vibrant reef systems that are reachable from numerous beaches throughout the archipelago. Here, you can go snorkeling with vibrant fish, amusing octopuses, and inquisitive reef sharks.

In the Seychelles, diving and snorkeling present an unmatched chance to discover this tropical paradise's underwater treasures. For both divers and snorkelers, the Seychelles offers an amazing underwater experience with its colorful coral reefs, abundant marine life, and unspoiled dive spots.

## Boating and Sailing

Seychelles is a sailor's paradise, offering sailing and yachting enthusiasts an unmatched experience with its dispersed islands and turquoise waters. The archipelago's mild trade winds, protected anchorages, and breathtaking scenery offer the ideal setting for an amazing nautical adventure, regardless of your level of experience.

Yachtsmen and sailors can go on island hopping excursions to discover the Seychelles' varied collection of granite and coral islands. Every location, from the recognizable silhouette of Mahé to the immaculate beaches of Praslin and the isolated atolls of the Outer Islands, has a distinct charm and allure that just begs to be explored.

Seychelles offers sailors and yachters a wealth of protected anchorages and immaculate bays where they can drop anchor and take in the peace and quiet of the islands. Every anchorage on the archipelago is picture-perfect, with serene waters and stunning scenery making it the ideal place to moor, whether you're exploring hidden coves on La Digue or Port Launay Marine Park.

The Seychelles are home to a number of up-to-date marinas, yacht clubs, and amenities for sailors and boaters, such as mooring spaces, provisioning services, and technical assistance. You'll find everything you need to ensure a smooth and pleasurable sailing or yachting adventure, whether you're docking at Eden Island Marina or anchoring in the quiet waters of Cousin Island.

Throughout the year, Seychelles organizes a range of sailing competitions and regattas that draw sailors and boaters from all over the world to partake in friendly races and commemorate the spirit of sailing. Participating in the Seychelles Regatta or Seychelles Round Race provides an exciting chance to meet other sailors and get a firsthand look at Seychelles' maritime culture.

The Seychelles provide an unmatched chance to experience the peace and beauty of this tropical haven from the water through sailing and yachting. For sailors and yachters of all ages and skill levels, the Seychelles offers an amazing maritime experience with its immaculate anchorages, top-notch sailing conditions, and dedication to marine conservation. Set out on a once-in-a-lifetime journey across the azure waters of the Seychelles by raising your sails and charting your course for adventure.

## Fishing Adventures

Seychelles' pristine waters, plethora of marine life, and varied fishing options draw anglers from all over the world to this unrivaled fishing destination in the middle of the Indian Ocean. Everyone who fishes in Seychelles is guaranteed an amazing experience, regardless of experience level.

Take a deep-sea fishing expedition offshore and throw your lines into the abundant waters surrounding the Seychelles. Sailfish, dorado, tuna, and marlin are among the highly sought-after game fish that you can target while exploring the deep blue waters to find the big one. Skilled charter operators guarantee a successful and exciting fishing experience by offering top-notch gear, professional advice, and insider knowledge of the best fishing spots.

Famous for its top-notch fly-fishing experiences, the Seychelles boasts shallow flats, lagoons, and reef systems that are abundant in bonefish, permit, and trevally. Either wade through glistening flats and sight-fish for elusive species in their natural environment, or go on a guided flats skiff fishing trip and stalk trophy fish in secluded, unspoiled areas.

Bottom fishing trips give anglers the opportunity to catch a range of reef-dwelling species, including snapper, grouper, and barracuda, for a more laid-back fishing experience. Drop your lines in close proximity to underwater structures, rock formations, and coral reefs to experience the exhilaration of engaging in combat with resilient fish while taking in the breathtaking coastal landscape of the Seychelles.

Seychelles has stringent laws in place to safeguard its delicate marine ecosystems and conserve fish stocks for future generations. The country is dedicated to sustainable fishing methods and marine conservation. To maintain the long-term health and sustainability of the marine resources in the Seychelles, anglers are urged to support local conservation initiatives, observe size and bag limits, and engage in catch-and-release fishing.

Anglers of all skill levels can enjoy the excitement of sport fishing in one of the most pristine and biodiverse marine environments on the planet by going on fishing excursions in the Seychelles. Casting your lines from the shoreline, stalking bonefish on the flats, or pursuing trophy fish offshore—the Seychelles promises an incredible fishing experience amidst stunning natural beauty and friendly Seychelloise hospitality.

### Trails for Hiking and Nature

Seychelles is well known for its gorgeous beaches and glistening waters, but it's also a hiking and nature lover's dream come true because of its abundance of lush rainforests, verdant valleys, and dramatic granite peaks. Explore the Seychelles' extensive network of hiking trails and nature reserves to go deeper into the rich biodiversity and stunning scenery of this archipelago.

Seychellois National Park, Morne, hiking trails for every skill level can be found in Morne Seychellois National Park, which is home to the highest peak in the Seychelles. Hike up granite slopes, through dense forests, and to the summit of Morne Blanc for expansive views of Mahe Island and beyond.

Nature Reserve of Vallée de Mai, explore the UNESCO World Heritage Site Valléee de Mai, which is home to the recognizable coco de mer palm, and its prehistoric wonders. Discover unique plants and animals that are unique to this place, stroll along paths that are shaded, and take in the symphony of birdsong.

Park Praslin National, explore the varied ecosystems of Praslin National Park by meandering through its winding trails, which lead past mangrove swamps, palm forests, granite outcrops, and isolated beaches. Explore the interior of this natural sanctuary and look for endemic bird species, such as the Seychelles black parrot.

Copolia Path, hiking Mahe Island's Copolia Trail is a demanding but worthwhile experience. Reach the summit, where you'll be rewarded with sweeping views of Mahe's coastline and neighboring islands after ascending through dense vegetation and past granite boulders.

In the Seychelles, hiking and nature trails present a singular chance to experience the natural beauty of the archipelago and discover its various ecosystems. Wandering along coastal pathways, climbing granite peaks, or trekking through ancient forests—the Seychelles offers an incredible experience amidst stunning scenery and a plethora of wildlife. Put on your hiking boots, remember to bring plenty of water and sunscreen, and set out on a discovery trip through the captivating Seychelles wilderness.

## Tours of Wildlife and Bird Watching

For those who enjoy watching birds and other wildlife, the Seychelles is a haven due to its abundant biodiversity and unspoiled natural environments. Discover the diverse array of fauna in the archipelago, which includes unique land and marine animals as well as endemic bird species just waiting to be discovered. Take a bird watching and wildlife tour in the Seychelles to discover the unspoiled wilderness of the islands and see rare and fascinating species in their natural habitat.

Numerous endemic bird species can be found in the Seychelles, such as the Seychelles black parrot, Seychelles blue pigeon, and Seychelles magpie robin. Take part in guided birdwatching tours to see these elusive birds and discover more about their behavior and state of conservation in places like Vallée de Mai and Cousin Island Special Reserve.

Engage in the diverse marine ecosystems of the Seychelles and come across a range of marine creatures, such as colorful reef fish, dolphins, and sea turtles. Explore mangrove forests, seagrass beds, and coral reefs with snorkeling and diving tours to see marine life in its natural environment.

Uncover the rich biodiversity of the Seychelles by visiting wildlife sanctuaries and reserves like Aride Island and Cousin Island. Discover pristine environments full of unique flora and fauna, such as rare seabirds, giant tortoises, and nesting turtles, and gain knowledge about conservation initiatives aimed at preserving these delicate ecosystems.

Take part in expertly guided wildlife tours conducted by naturalist guides with extensive knowledge of the flora and fauna of the Seychelles. Discover the various habitats of the islands and come across uncommon and intriguing species as you travel around, gaining knowledge about the ecology, behavior, and conservation of the Seychelles' wildlife.

Seychelles wildlife tours and bird watching provide a comprehensive understanding of the archipelago's ecological diversity and natural beauty. Seychelles promises an amazing experience for nature lovers of all ages, whether you're seeing rare birds in lush rainforests, snorkeling alongside marine life in crystal-clear waters, or exploring wildlife reserves teeming with endemic species. So gather your sense of wonder, a camera, and binoculars and set out on a journey to explore the fascinating wildlife of the Seychelles.

# Chapter 7

# Cultural Encounters

Take in the vibrant tapestry of Seychellois culture, where each encounter narrates a tale of warm hospitality and rich heritage. Seychelles offers a kaleidoscope of cultural experiences just waiting to be discovered, from vibrant Creole markets brimming with spices and crafts to traditional dance performances that echo the rhythms of the islands. Savor mouthwatering Creole cuisine, which combines flavors from Asia, Europe, and Africa to create dishes that will entice your senses and leave you wanting more. Discover the fascinating history of the Seychelles through visiting historic sites and museums that tell tales of piracy and trade, as well as colonial influences. Interact with regional craftspeople, discover age-old methods that have been passed down through the generations, and bring home one-of-a-kind mementos that perfectly encapsulate Seychellois craftsmanship.

# Local Delights and Creole Cuisine

The Seychelles is a culinary haven with a rich tapestry of flavors influenced by African, French, Indian, and Chinese cuisines, in addition to being a paradise for its breathtaking natural beauty. Creole cuisine, a synthesis of various cultures and customs that honors the islands' distinct cultural identity, is at the core of Seychellois culinary heritage.

Flavors of Creole Fusion, bold flavors, spicy spices, and fresh ingredients from both the sea and the land define Seychelles' creole cuisine. A symphony of flavors that entice the palate is often created in dishes by combining herbs, spices, coconut milk, and tropical fruits in a harmonious manner.

The cuisine of Seychelles is known for its signature dishes, which include "Caris" (creole curries) that are made with fish, meat, or vegetables simmered in a fragrant sauce made of coconut milk, "Rousettes" (fruit bat curry) for the more daring diner, and "Ladob" (a dessert made with ripe plantains or breadfruit cooked in coconut milk and sugar).

The Seychelles, with its wealth of marine resources, has an abundance of delectable fresh seafood dishes, such as "Grilled Fish" with a spicy Creole sauce, "Octopus Salad" with lime and chili marinade, and "Bourzwa" (sea urchin) for a distinct ocean flavor.

Savor regional delicacies like "Samosas" stuffed with fiery meat or veggies, "Bouillon Bred" (breadfruit chips) drenched in tart tamarind sauce, and "Takamaka Rum" flavored with spices and tropical fruits. Discover the Seychelles' thriving street food scene.

The Creole cuisine of the Seychelles is influenced by a variety of cultures, including African, Indian, Chinese, and European culinary customs. Every dish, from flavorful chutneys and pickles to fragrant curries, reflects the multicultural heritage of the Seychelles.

Take part in market tours, seafood feasts prepared by regional chefs, and Creole cooking classes to fully immerse yourself in Seychellois culture. Participate in community activities, pick up traditional cooking methods, and learn the recipes for the most popular Seychelles dishes.

In the Seychelles, local specialties and creole cuisine provide a culinary adventure into the core of the rich cultural legacy of the islands. Every bite of food is a celebration of the vibrant flavors and traditions of the Seychelles, whether you're cooking with Seychellois chefs, eating at a restaurant by the sea, or both. Come hungry and get ready to indulge in the delectable flavors of Creole cuisine in this idyllic tropical setting.

### Customary Dance and Music

The colorful history and diverse heritage of the archipelago of Seychelles are reflected in the lively threads of traditional music and dance that weave together its cultural tapestry. Seychellois music and dance, which celebrate the joys, sorrows, and rhythms of daily life, are an essential part of the islands' cultural identity and have their roots in African, European, and Asian influences.

Sega Dance and Music, the most famous dance style in the Seychelles is the Sega, which is distinguished by its upbeat melodies, swaying hips, and rhythmic beats. The Sega, which originated from African slaves that French and British colonists brought to the islands, has come to represent Seychelles identity. Its upbeat rhythms and energetic movements enthrall audiences at festivals, weddings, and social events.

Moutya Drumming, another traditional music and dance style from the Seychelles is called moutya, and it's distinguished by its expressive movements and hypnotic drumming rhythms. Moutya, which was first performed by slaves as a means of resistance and self-expression, has developed into a cultural art form that honors the tenacity and spirit of the Seychellois people.

Polka and Kontredans, the traditional music and dance of the Seychelles is heavily influenced by Europe, dances like the Polka and Kontredans are remnants of the islands' colonial past. These vibrant and graceful dances highlight the Seychelles' multicultural heritage and cosmopolitan flair and are frequently performed at formal events and cultural gatherings.

Orchestras and Instruments, a range of instruments, such as the triangle, the maracas, and the tambour, a large drum played with sticks, are used to accompany traditional Seychellois music. Local ensembles that combine traditional and modern styles produce lively, varied shows that enthrall audiences of all ages.

African, European, and Asian influences are blended to create a distinctive and dynamic art form in Seychelles traditional music and dance, which is a vibrant expression of the islands' rich cultural heritage. The traditional music and dance scene of the Seychelles promises an amazing cultural experience that will stay with you forever, whether you're dancing the night away at a Kontredans, swaying to the beat of the Sega, or being enthralled by the beat of the Moutya drum.

## Handmade Items and Memorabilia

In addition to being a haven for lovers of the outdoors, the Seychelles are a veritable gold mine of handcrafted goods that showcase the islands' vivid inventiveness and rich cultural legacy. Seychellois craftspeople create a wide range of traditional and modern items that honor the archipelago's distinct identity, from colorful textiles and distinctive jewelry to deftly woven baskets and hand-carved sculptures.

The traditional Creole baskets of Seychelles are well-known, painstakingly crafted from indigenous materials like vetiver grass, pandanus leaves, and coconut palms. These exquisitely made baskets are available in a range of sizes and shapes, and their elaborate patterns and designs pay homage to the rich cultural legacy of the Seychelles.

Coconut Shell Creation, Seychelles artisans craft everything from finely carved jewelry and ornaments to ornamental bowls and utensils out of ordinary coconut shells. Each of these one-of-a-kind pieces tells a tale of island life and the breathtaking natural surroundings, showcasing the Seychelles' inventiveness and resourcefulness.

The Seychelles' native artisans are well known for their exquisite wood carvings and sculptures that portray island life, marine life, and local flora and fauna. These finely carved works of art, which range in size from small figurines and masks to enormous sculptures, highlight the artistic talent and cultural diversity of the Seychelles.

The natural beauty and rich cultural legacy of the Seychelles serve as inspiration for the diverse textiles and embroidery created by Seychelles artisans. These handcrafted textiles, which range from vibrant batik fabrics and sarongs to embroidered tablecloths and cushion covers, give any room or outfit a dash of Seychellois flair.

Uncover distinctive accessories and jewelry influenced by the marine life and natural scenery of the Seychelles. These handcrafted pieces, which range from seashell necklaces and coral earrings to beaded bracelets and pearl jewelry, perfectly capture the natural beauty and exotic charm of the Seychelles.

Seychelles artisanal goods and souvenirs present a special chance to bring home a bit of the islands' rich cultural legacy and breathtaking scenery. The Seychelles' handcrafted goods, such as eco-friendly jewelry, hand-carved sculptures, and traditional Creole baskets, ensure that your island vacation will be remembered for its genuine and unforgettable quality.

## Celebrations and Occasions

The Seychelles is a bustling location that hosts numerous festivals and events all year long to celebrate its rich heritage and cultural diversity. The island chain offers a varied schedule of events that highlight Seychellois customs, music, and culture, from vibrant carnivals and music festivals to customary rituals and religious celebrations.

Festival of Creole, one of the most eagerly awaited occasions in Seychelles is the Creole Festival, a week-long celebration of music, dance, food, and the arts that honors the islands' Creole culture. Immerse yourself in Creole customs, take in live performances by regional musicians, eat traditional food, and peruse handcrafted goods at the lively street markets.

Carnaval International de Victoria, held in the Seychelles, the Carnaval International de Victoria is a grand celebration of diversity and culture that includes street acts, vibrant parades, and international cultural exhibitions. With participants from many nations showcasing their distinct customs and heritage, the capital city of Victoria is transformed into a vibrant and joyous place.

Victoria's Seychelles International Carnival, the colorful and lively Seychelles International Carnival of Victoria unites people from all over the world to celebrate the unity and diversity of the Seychelles islands' cultures. The carnival culminates in a magnificent procession through Victoria's streets and includes street parties, vibrant floats, and traditional music and dance performances.

Kreol Festival, every October, Festival Kreol honors the culture and legacy of the Creole people. The festival offers a broad array of activities, such as craft fairs, cooking demos, traditional music and dance performances, and cultural exhibitions showcasing the distinctive Creole identity of the Seychelles.

Seychelles festivals and events present a singular chance to get a firsthand look at the lively music, culture, and customs of the islands. Seychelles festivals promise an amazing celebration of island life and cultural diversity, whether you're dancing in the streets at the Creole Festival, taking in the vibrant floats at the Carnaval International de Victoria, or indulging in traditional cuisine at the Festival Kreol.

# Chapter 8

# Useful Information

Discover the keys to a flawless Seychelles trip with our helpful advice! We have everything you need, from must-have travel documents to dos and don'ts when exchanging currencies. Discover the island's best-kept secrets with our insider transportation advice, eat like a local with our restaurant suggestions, and easily stay connected while enjoying the sun. Whether you're traveling alone or organizing a family vacation, our useful advice guarantees a worry-free and amazing time in paradise. With all the information you need to ensure a smooth travel experience from beginning to end, get ready to explore the wonders of the Seychelles!

# Money and Transaction

A seamless and pleasurable trip to this tropical haven requires familiarity with currency and payment procedures in the Seychelles.

"SR" or "SCR" stands for the Seychellois Rupee (SCR), the official currency of the Seychelles. There are five different denominations of banknotes: 25, 50, 100, and 500 rupees, coins have denominations of 1, 5, and 10 rupees.

Check the exchange rates from your home currency to the Seychellois Rupee before your trip. It's wise to compare rates at banks, currency exchange offices, and even your hotel as exchange rates can differ depending on where you exchange your money.

It is generally a good idea to have some cash on hand for smaller purchases and transactions, even though credit and debit cards are widely accepted at hotels, restaurants, and larger establishments in the Seychelles. The most widely accepted credit and debit cards are Visa and Mastercard, though some establishments may also accept American Express and Diners Club.

In Seychelles, you can easily find ATMs in popular towns and tourist destinations, where you can take out cash in local currency. To avoid any problems, check with your bank about international withdrawal fees and let them know about your travel schedule. It's crucial to remember that some ATMs might have withdrawal limits or impose additional fees.

It's best to exchange money at banks, exchange bureaus, or other respectable locations to guarantee you get a reasonable exchange rate. Steer clear of street vendors and unofficial sources when exchanging money because they might offer bad rates or fake money.

For your visit to be hassle-free, it is imperative that you comprehend currency and payment methods in the Seychelles. You can enjoy your time in the Seychelles with confidence if you are well-prepared to manage your finances responsibly and effectively by becoming familiar with the local currency, exchange rates, accepted payment methods, and tipping customs.

## Speech and Hearing

Seychelles' multilingual population and varied cultural legacy are reflected in the language and communication of the archipelago.

Languages that are Official, English, French, and Seychellois Creole are the three official languages of the Seychelles. The language most commonly spoken by Seychellois of all ethnic backgrounds, Seychellois Creole—often simply called Creole, serves as their common language. In business, government, and education, people speak English, but in travel and tourism, people speak French.

Seychellois Creole Language, African, French, and English influences have combined to create the distinctive language known as creole. Its expressive gestures, vibrant vocabulary, and melodic rhythm are its defining characteristics. Although Creole and English are widely understood, knowing a few basic phrases in the language can improve your interactions with locals and broaden your cultural experience.

English and French are widely spoken among Seychelles, especially in cities and popular tourist destinations. In hotels, restaurants, and tourist destinations, most people speak English, but in hospitality and customer service roles, most people speak French. People of African, European, and Asian descent make up the diverse population of the Seychelles. This cultural diversity enhances the Seychelles' linguistic and communicative environment and fosters harmony and inclusivity in a community that values diversity in language and customs.

The Seychelles' varied population and rich cultural legacy are reflected in the language and communication used there. Learn a few basic phrases in Creole, become conversant in the official languages, and engage in courteous communication to improve your cultural immersion and build lasting relationships with the friendly and hospitable people of the Seychelles.

## Services and Contacts for Emergencies

It is important to plan ahead for any unforeseen emergencies that may occur when visiting a new location. Having an understanding of emergency contacts and services can ease your mind and guarantee prompt assistance when needed.

Emergency Numbers, Police: In the event of an emergency, such as a theft, assault, or criminal activity, dial 999 for prompt assistance.

Ambulance: In case of an accident, injury, or sudden illness requiring immediate medical attention, dial 999.

Fire Brigade: To report a fire or any other incident requiring the use of firefighting services, dial 999.

Medical Facilities, Infirmaries and Clinics: Find the closest medical facilities—clinics, hospitals, etc.—in your neighborhood. Hospitals in the Seychelles that offer emergency medical care include the Seychelles Hospital in Victoria on Mahé Island.

Medicines: Make a note of the hours that the local pharmacies are open. Essential pharmaceuticals and medical supplies are available in Seychelles pharmacies.

Consulate or Embassy: Locate the phone number and address of the embassy or consulate of your nation in the Seychelles. They can help you with consular support emergencies, legal matters, and passport issues.

Travel Insurance Details and Information, Policy Specifics: Keep a copy of your travel insurance policy on you, along with the coverage details and emergency contact information.

Medical Coverage: Verify that your travel insurance offers complete medical coverage, including emergency medical evacuation in the event that it becomes necessary.

Tourist Information Centers: Consult visitor bureaus or tourist information centers for advice on nearby services, sights, and emergency support.

Hotels and Lodgings: In the event of an emergency, let the personnel at your hotel or place of lodging know. In the event that you need it, they can offer advice and make emergency service calls.

Taxis and Public Transportation: To get to medical facilities or emergency services fast, use authorized taxis or public transportation.

Rental Cars: In the event of an accident, a breakdown, or other vehicle-related emergency, call the emergency hotline provided by the rental company.

Having a plan and knowing who to call in case of emergency and other services is crucial to a pleasant and safe trip. While visiting the Seychelles or any other location, you can effectively handle emergencies and ensure your well-being by being informed and taking proactive steps.

# Chapter 9

# Sample of Itineraries

With the help of our carefully planned sample itineraries, set out on an amazing voyage through the Seychelles! Whether your travel style is adventure, romance, or relaxation, we have the ideal itinerary. As you tour the islands, enjoy the flavors of Creole cuisine, hike beautiful trails, and dive into crystal-clear waters. Experience the natural beauty and lively culture of the Seychelles while indulging in opulent resorts or opting for more affordable options. Our sample itineraries give you an idea of the variety of experiences this tropical paradise has to offer, from island hopping to cultural events. So gather your belongings and get ready for an incredible journey to the Seychelles!

## A 7-Day Adventure of Island Hopping

Take part in the ultimate 7-day island hopping adventure in the Seychelles, where there are endless wonders and treasures to uncover every day. This is a detailed schedule to help you get the most out of your trip to the Seychelles:

Day 1: Getting to Mahé

Once you reach Mahé, the main island of Seychelles, take a seat in your lodging. Take a day to tour Victoria, the nation's capital, taking in sights such as the Botanical Gardens, the Sir Selwyn Selwyn-Clarke Market, and the Clock Tower.

Day 2: Discovery of the Mahé Islands

Explore Mahé's breathtaking beaches, verdant rainforests, and expansive vistas during a full-day island tour. Explore well-known locations for hiking and wildlife observation, such as Beau Vallon Beach, Anse Intendance, and the Morne Seychellois National Park.

Day 3: Praxin to Ferry

Praslin, which is renowned for its immaculate beaches and the Valle de Mai Nature Reserve, is reachable by ferry. Enjoy a leisurely day exploring the prehistoric Valle de Mai forest, snorkeling in the crystal-clear waters, and lounging on Anse Lazio Beach.

Day 4: La Digue Adventure

Take a ferry to the quaint island of La Digue, which is well-known for its relaxed atmosphere and recognizable granite rocks. Embark on a leisurely bicycle tour of the island, stopping at sites such as Anse Source d'Argent, Grand Anse, and L'Union Estate.

Day 5: Island Exploration on Silhouette

Take a day excursion to Silhouette Island, a pristine nature reserve renowned for its quiet beaches and verdant forests. Relax on the quiet beaches of Anse Lascars, take a hike to Mount Dauban for sweeping views, and go snorkeling in the marine sanctuary.

Day 6: Immersion in Mahé Culture

Go back to Mahé and experience the culture of the Seychelles firsthand. Discover the lively culture of the islands by going to local markets, eating at Creole eateries, and seeing a traditional music and dance show.

Day 7: Leaving

With lifelong memories, bid the Seychelles farewell. Take with you the enchantment and splendor of the Seychelles islands as you depart from Mahé International Airport.

On this incredible 7-day island hopping excursion, take in the best of the Seychelles' natural beauty, culture, and adventure.

## Romantic Vacation for Couples

Enjoy a romantic getaway for two in the stunning Seychelles, where powdery beaches, turquoise waters, and lush scenery create the perfect setting for an amazing trip with your significant other.

Day 1: Getting to Mahé
Welcomed with breathtaking views and gracious hospitality, Mahé is the main island of the Seychelles. Once at your opulent beachfront resort, unwind with a couples massage at the spa or spend the day relaxing by the infinity pool, which offers panoramic views of the ocean.

Day 2: Exclusive Beach Picnic
In the seclusion of your villa or on the beach, begin your day with a leisurely breakfast. Explore secret beaches and quiet coves with your partner during the morning. Savor a romantic beach picnic in the afternoon, catered by your resort and complete with fine foods and bubbly.

Day 3: Cruise at Sunset
Sail around Mahé or its nearby islands at sunset for a chance to take in the stunning scenery of the coastline as the sun sets. As the sky bursts into brilliant pink, orange, and gold hues, sip champagne and feast on fresh seafood.

Day 4: Island Touring

Together, set out to discover the Seychelles' natural splendor. Experience the serene Jardin du Roi Spice Garden for a romantic stroll, go swimming in the pristine waters of Anse Intendance, or go on a guided hike through the lush rainforests of Morne Seychellois National Park.

Day 5: Exclusive Beachside Dinner

Enjoy a romantic dinner on the beach beneath the stars while holding a candlelit conversation. As you savor a gourmet feast of fresh seafood and Creole specialties, you'll be lulled by the sound of the gentle sea breeze and the breaking waves.

Day 6: La Digue Tour

Take a ferry to the quaint island of La Digue, where you can experience a time warp. Rent bicycles and ride around the island's hidden beaches, such as the well-known Anse Source d'Argent, which is known for its immaculate sands and towering granite boulders.

Day 7: Leaving

With treasured memories of your romantic getaway, bid the Seychelles farewell. As you depart from Mahé International Airport, make a promise to yourself to return to this enchanted paradise for a number of future romantic retreats.

Take your special someone on a romantic getaway to discover the wonders of the Seychelles, complete with breathtaking scenery, unforgettable moments, and countless chances for romance and relaxation.

## A Fun Vacation with the Family

Is a family vacation amidst breathtaking beaches, verdant surroundings, and lively culture on your bucket list? Seychelles is the only place to look! 115 islands make up the Seychelles archipelago, which is tucked away in the Indian Ocean and provides visitors of all ages with the ideal mix of adventure and leisure.

Although the Seychelles has a warm, tropical climate all year round, the dry season, which runs from May to September, is the ideal time to take a family vacation because of the lower temperatures and reduced humidity. To enjoy less crowds and better prices on lodging and activities, think about avoiding the busiest travel months of December through February.

Seek out resorts or hotels that are ideal for families, with features like roomy villas or rooms, kid-friendly pools, and well-supervised kids' clubs. Numerous resorts in the Seychelles offer extra services to keep kids occupied while parents unwind, like kid-friendly menus, babysitting, and family-friendly activities.

Mahé, the largest island, has calm beaches ideal for swimming and snorkeling, such as Beau Vallon, that are family-friendly.

With its easy hiking trails and chances to see rare plants and animals, Praslin, the location of the UNESCO-listed Vallée de Mai, is a wonderful family destination for those who enjoy the outdoors.

La Digue is the perfect place to go on bike adventures with the kids because of its famous Anse Source d'Argent beach and relaxed atmosphere.

Make memories with your family by having picnics on the immaculate beaches of the Seychelles, collecting seashells, and building sandcastles. In the calm, crystal-clear waters of the Indian Ocean, try family-friendly water sports like paddleboarding, kayaking, and snorkeling.

Explore the rich biodiversity of the Seychelles with your children on an unforgettable eco-adventure. Take guided hikes and see wildlife at nature reserves like the Fond Ferdinand Nature Reserve on Praslin or the Morne Seychellois National Park on Mahé. Don't pass up the opportunity to take your kids on guided tours or visits to conservation centers where they can learn about the endemic bird species, colorful marine life, and massive tortoises of the Seychelles.

Take your family on a culinary adventure, visit local markets, or attend live cultural events to fully immerse them in Seychellois culture.

In family-friendly eateries and seaside cafes, treat your kids to mouthwatering Creole fare, such as succulent seafood, vibrant fruits, and aromatic curries.

Make sure you take lots of pictures and videos so you can look back on your family's wonderful vacation in the Seychelles for years to come.

To capture their memories and experiences of the Seychelles, encourage your kids to keep a scrapbook or travel journal.

Families will find countless chances to connect, explore, and make enduring memories in the idyllic tropical setting of the Seychelles. Your family-friendly trip to the Seychelles will undoubtedly be an amazing experience full of joy, exploration, and rest if you approach it with thoughtful planning and a spirit of adventure.

# Conclusion

When the sun sets on your virtual voyage through the captivating Seychelles islands, it's appropriate to pause and consider the plethora of experiences and revelations that await visitors to this idyllic tropical location. Everyone who visits the Seychelles is enthralled by its turquoise waters, verdant rainforests, and lively culture.

We've covered all the details of organizing your trip to the Seychelles in this extensive travel guide, from figuring out when to go to discovering the wide range of activities and sights dispersed throughout the archipelago's islands. Travelers seeking adventure in wild nature, relaxation on immaculate beaches, or cultural immersion will find something to suit their needs in the Seychelles.

The Seychelles offer a journey of experiences ready to be woven into your travel narrative, from the busy streets of Mahé, the capital city, to the quiet coves of La Digue. Explore the islands' rich history and culture, which are influenced by French, African, and Asian cultures to produce a distinctive and colorful tapestry of customs, food, and traditions.

Take on eco-adventures through verdant national parks, home to protected sanctuaries where endemic wildlife and plants flourish. Hike along picturesque trails to hidden waterfalls and expansive views, or jump into the glistening clear waters teeming with colorful marine life.

Savor the flavors of Seychelles cuisine, which combines mouthwatering seafood, unusual fruits, and flavorful spices to create a harmonious blend of flavors. Try some local markets' specialties, or eat outside on the beach beneath the stars. Every meal entices visitors to experience the spirit of the islands by narrating a tale from the rich cultural past of the Seychelles.

Seychelles is a model of sustainability and conservation, though its stunning beauty and mouth watering cuisine go far beyond that. Keep in mind to tread carefully as you explore its pristine ecosystems and show respect for the delicate natural balance that keeps life on these islands. Select environmentally conscious lodging, contribute to nearby conservation initiatives, and only leave trace evidence of your visit to ensure that the Seychelles is preserved as a sanctuary for future generations.

Seychelles is a journey of exploration, renewal, and reconnection with nature rather than just a place to visit. The Seychelles extends an invitation to set out on a once-in-a-lifetime journey, catering to your desires of adventure, leisure, or cultural exposure.

Printed in Great Britain
by Amazon